CHRISTMAS

THE GOOD, THE BAD, AND THE UGLY

An Advent Study for Adults

Richard B. Wilke

Abingdon Press
Nashville

CHRISTMAS
THE GOOD, THE BAD, AND THE UGLY

Copyright © 2010 by Abingdon Press

Library of Congress Cataloging-in-Publication Data

Wilke, Richard B., 1930-
    Christmas—the good, the bad, and the ugly : an Advent study for adults / Richard B. Wilke.
       p.   cm.
    ISBN 978-0-687-66034-6 (trade pbk. : alk. paper)
    1. Advent—Meditations. I. Title.
    BV40.W52 2010
    242'.33—dc22

                                                                                    2010016244

Scripture quotations, unless otherwise noted, are from the New Revised Standard Version of the Bible, copyright 1989, Division of Christian Education of the National Council of the Churches of Christ in the United States of America. Used by permission. All rights reserved.

Scripture quotations marked NIV are taken from the Holy Bible, NEW INTERNATIONAL VERSION®. Copyright © 1973, 1978, 1984 by International Bible Society. All rights reserved throughout the world. Used by permission of International Bible Society.

Scripture quotations marked RSV are taken from the Revised Standard Version of the Bible, copyright 1952 [2nd edition, 1971] by the Division of Christian Education of the National Council of the Churches of Christ in the United States of America. Used by permission. All rights reserved.

10 11 12 13 14 15 16 17 18 19—10 9 8 7 6 5 4 3 2 1
MANUFACTURED IN THE UNITED STATES OF AMERICA

Contents

INTRODUCTION

CHRISTMAS IS SO SPECIAL!

Central to the sacred ceremony, of course, stands the birth of our Savior. "For to us a child is born, to us a son is given, and the government will be on his shoulders" (Isaiah 9:6 NIV). Every birth is important, but the One who healed the sick, fed the hungry, and held children in his arms, the One who died on the cross for our sins and for the sins of the whole world—his birth must be celebrated with celestial joy and reverential awe.

Our faith demands that we focus on the birth of our Lord Jesus at Christmas. Do you remember when George Beverly Shea used to sing "Put Christ Back into Christmas"? Amid the swirl of Christmas tree ornaments and the frenzy of holiday shopping, that song reminds us to keep our central focus on the Babe of Bethlehem.

But I have also discovered that the people and events encircling the holy birth have powerful spiritual meanings of their own. Not only do we kneel before the manger in faithful adoration of our Savior, but we notice those persons surrounding the blessed baby: shepherds and wise men, Mary and Joseph, angels and the innkeeper—even the evil King Herod—and we learn from them too.

Years ago, as pastor of a downtown city church, I talked with Sunday school teachers and youth workers who were worn out with putting on the annual Christmas pageant. They were weary of fussy babies and restless children, tired of boy "shepherds" dueling like the three musketeers with their shepherds' crooks during practices. They abandoned the simple children's Christmas program—laid it to rest. They said, "Let the choir sing a classical cantata instead." Thus, no Christmas pageant was held for several years.

Some time later, one morning in early November, three or four young mothers came into my study. They said they had a wonderful idea. They wanted to help children portray the Christmas story. Their eyes glistened with excitement as they explained, "We could have some ten-year-old boys go barefoot or wear sandals and be shepherds! We could have older boys, even girls, dress up in bathrobes and crowns and be wise men! A teenage girl could be Mary; a friend just had a baby, whom Mary might hold!" Those young women were as enthused as children opening early-morning presents under the Christmas tree. I kept a straight face, not knowing whether to laugh or cry, as they, in their innocence, dreamed of presenting an all-church Christmas pageant, as if one had never been done before.

Then I realized that those young mothers were hungry to experience the powerful spiritual symbolism of the manger scene. Amid the dangers of Christmas being merely a mad rush to the mall, the household stress of decorating a tree, and wrapping presents, they wanted to remember Bethlehem. They wanted children to know the true Christmas story and to learn more about Jesus. So we held a beautiful Christmas pageant—and we remembered!

So we remember now, as we look at some of the different parts of the story. Even some that we tend to hope to forget.

—Richard B. Wilke

LET'S KEEP HEROD IN CHRISTMAS

Scripture: Read Matthew 2:1, 7-8, 16-18.

Herod, the Man Who Tried to Kill Christmas

HEROD "THE GREAT," as he was known, was a bad man; a cruel man; an evil man. Here is some background. He was born in the deserts of Sinai, a descendant of Abraham through Esau (or Edom). The Edomites, later known as Idumaeans, had been forcibly converted to Judaism by the Maccabees, who led the revolt that freed Judea from Syrian rule, so the Idumaeans were not descended from historically Jewish families. Thus Herod and his people were known as Edomite Jews.

The world was in turmoil. In Rome, Brutus and Cassius had murdered Julius Caesar. In the struggle for power, Cassius was defeated by Mark Antony, who was killed by Octavian—who later became known as Caesar Augustus, the first ruler of the newly named Roman Empire. Rome was trying to subjugate and control Greece, the Near East, and Egypt. Rome needed help governing Palestine.

The Hasmoneans, a Dynasty descended from the Maccabees, were the Jewish high priests and kings who ruled Israel from 143 to 37 B.C.;

but the dynasty grew weak due to infighting, and Herod's father, Antipater, who allied himself with the Roman leadership, was named ruler of Judea. Herod, a young soldier, charismatic, adept with javelin and bow, was sent to Rome to build friends among key Roman leaders. Later he was dispatched to become governor of Galilee. He proved to be a friend of Rome by brutally crushing a local Jewish rebellion. Herod became expert at playing both ends against the middle.

When Herod's father was poisoned, Rome named Herod ruler of Judea. To solidify his authority, Herod married Mariamne, a beautiful Hasmonean princess whose father was the High Priest Hyrcanus. Eventually Herod had a number of wives to solidify political ties, but Mariamne was his favorite. He loved her insanely; he was passionately jealous. When she urged him to appoint her brother Aristobulus as high priest, he did so. But Herod had the popular Aristobulus, who was only seventeen, drowned within a year, and his mother blamed Herod. (The emperor Augustus is reported to have said at some point, "It is safer to be Herod's pig than to be his son.") Mariamne accused Herod of killing both her brother and her grandfather. Herod's sister, Salome, told Herod that Mariamne was sleeping with an uncle, so, according to Jewish historian Josephus, Herod ordered Mariamne's execution.

Herod was brutal. He wanted absolute control. He murdered important Hasmoneans, Pharisees, and priests of the ruling body, the Sanhedrin, while installing "yes men" in their places. So by the time the wise men came to Jerusalem, it was Herod's men who served as the elders. And Herod reduced their power by continually changing high priests.

Herod pacified most of the Jewish people under his rule by allowing them to worship their God in the Temple, instead of worshiping Caesar. In return, he placated Rome by demanding a huge temple tax, then sending that vast wealth to Rome. He kept the international trade routes open—incense from Yemen, olive oil from Galilee—with crushing taxes, again forwarding great wealth to Rome. Any uprising, he quashed brutally.

Herod, in part to elevate his own name, was a great builder. He lavishly remodeled the second Temple, with a solid gold altar, magnificent imported marble walls, and a beautiful "heavenly" blue ceiling. The Temple was so magnificent that millions of Jews, scattered all over the Mediterranean, returned to worship and admire. (This temple is the one Jesus visited. The Temple and all Jerusalem were destroyed by the Romans following an uprising in A.D. 70.)

To pacify Rome, Herod built a golden Roman eagle, placing it at the temple entrance. Some of the Jews became angry and tore the eagle down—its presence in the Temple being a sacrilege, they believed. Herod had the young men captured, placed in chains, dragged the thirteen miles down "The Valley of the Shadow of Death" from Jerusalem to Jericho, and burned alive.

To honor himself, Herod built a mountain, over two thousand feet high, near Jerusalem. He constructed a palace on top, which made it higher and taller than the Temple. He modestly named it the "Herodium." He also built the great Western Wall as part of the temple complex—the ruins of which are known by some today as the Wailing Wall. The platform, the size of 150 football fields, took ten thousand men ten years to build.

Herod built a huge seaport and named it Caesarea Maritima—which made the Romans happy, but not the Jews. (It stimulated trade but carried Caesar's name.) He also built amphitheaters for Greek and Roman theater and games, giving the people jobs but offending Jewish religious teachings.

Suspicion, fear, brutality, and jealousy permeated Herod's life and rule. He was considered to be an old man for those times, nearly seventy years old after forty years of ruthless rule, when the wise men came to Jerusalem. Matthew's Gospel tells the story. Those pilgrims inflamed his paranoia when they said they were looking for a baby who would become "king of the Jews." Herod's perverse mind flew into high gear as

9

he lied to the wise men, saying that he too wanted to go to Bethlehem, to worship the baby. He sent the wise men to Bethlehem and ordered them to return to him afterward, so that he could learn of the infant Jesus' location. But after visiting the baby Jesus in Bethlehem, the wise men, "having been warned in a dream not to return to Herod, . . . left for their own country by another road" (Matthew 2:12). Herod "was infuriated" (2:16) and, to stop the threat of losing his kingship to this newborn baby, "he sent and killed all the children in and around Bethlehem who were two years old or under" (2:16).

Just picture the soldiers breaking down the doors of every house in Bethlehem, killing all the babies right in their mothers' arms. The Bible explodes in grief. It recalls Rachel, wife of Jacob, who died in childbirth. She had become the generic term for women in tragedy. You can visit Rachel's tomb near Bethlehem, even today. You can weep and remember the children who were "no more" (Matthew 2:17-18).

At the time Jesus was born, Herod the Great was a seventy-year-old man plagued with illness and incessant family disputes involving his ten wives and fifteen children. Ancient sources like Josephus claim that, in his old age, Herod's illness grew steadily worse, complicated by high fever, intolerable itching, and inflammation of the abdomen. Herod's suspicious temperament and ruthless determination to remove any possible opposition intensified. Obsessed and paranoid, he had another son executed, Antipater, son of Herod's wife Doris. When he realized his own death was near, Herod ordered the arrest of all the leading citizens of all the villages. Then they were to be slaughtered at the moment of the king's death—thus tears would be shed and the nation would be plunged into mourning, even if not for him. Mercifully, his sister Salome countermanded the order, and all were later released.

Historians say that Herod was a godless man, reckless, willing to slay young or old, relative, friend, or enemy, showing no mercy.

Across the centuries, Herod the king has become a symbol of evil. We may rather want to forget that he is part of the Christmas story. But let's keep Herod in Christmas to remind us how desperately we need a Savior in this evil world.

Evil

Some folks think that evil is long ago and far away, like Nero feeding Christians to the lions in Rome or Hitler herding millions of people into the gas chambers in Europe. But with today's lightning-quick communications, we learn quickly of brutality, cruelty, deception, and crime, at home and around the world. At almost any given time, it seems, the headline news will tell us of a governor who was caught sleeping with a prostitute, a senator who has lied and cheated on personal income taxes, a corporate executive who has scammed billions of dollars from stockholders.

Evil around the globe crashes into our living rooms. A dictator in Zimbabwe grabs land and seals off the water that brings life to it, causing hundreds of thousands to die of starvation and cholera. Young Palestinian terrorists strap dynamite around their waists, blowing themselves up in a crowded Jerusalem mall. In return, Israeli planes bomb Palestinian schools and places of worship. Civil strife in Sudan slaughters thousands of women and children.

I live in a peaceful little town in Kansas. The police called me the other day: a woman who clerked at the local store was using our credit card number to gain money to buy drugs. Last week an alcoholic driver drank two bottles of vodka and ran over and killed a young mother with her four-year-old daughter. In a nearby town, a young man stalked, raped, and murdered a high school cheerleader. There is evil in the world.

The Bible says that evil is not "out there"; it's "in here." Evil is not limited to the Herods and Hitlers of history; evil resides in the human heart, like dormant seeds in fertile soil, ready to sprout and grow when given the opportunity.

Adam and Eve dramatize rebellion from the beginning. Instead of God's way, they did it their way. Their farmer son, Cain, murdered his rancher brother, Abel. Biblical history and all human history is replete with evil and its consequences. Scripture tells us that we have all sinned and fallen short of the glory of God (Romans 3:23). You and I are to pray, "forgive us our sins, for we ourselves forgive everyone indebted to us" (Luke 11:4).

Humankind is desperate for a Savior—a person of God powerful enough to save us from our sins, not only to forgive our iniquities but to turn our hearts from selfish self-seeking toward God in trust and compassion for others.

We desperately need more than just another prophet; we crave more than a good teacher; we must have better than a great physician. Like a drowning person crying for help, we plead for a Savior—for One who can save us from evil, turn us from our sinful selves, root out the "Herod" from our hearts.

Christmas is the fulcrum of history: Bethlehem marks the encounter between God's goodness and man's inhumanity to man, between salvation and self-centered sin, between God and evil, between the Savior and a satanic Herod.

Christmas Eve

My dad owned a funeral home with an emergency ambulance. I was fourteen years old, young, strong, restless—so Dad put me to work, lifting a cot or carrying a body to the embalming room. Doing this work, I saw something of the seamy side of life. On a rainy night, a drunken man crashed his car into a family van; an angry man shot his wife with a shotgun, then turned it on himself; and a child was left in a car to die of heat exhaustion. I saw the results of much evil.

Around that same time, the Battle of the Bulge—a major German offensive near the end of World War II—raged in Europe. I went with Dad to the railroad station to pick up the bodies of dead American soldiers— sometimes the father or older brother of a friend of mine. So on this particular Christmas Eve, I was depressed. Even at Grandma's house, with a room full of family laughing and opening presents, I was, understandably, withdrawn and blue.

I knew that the tiny Episcopal church two blocks away was holding Christmas Eve Holy Communion. No one else wanted to go, so I walked up the street, alone, discouraged, hoping to find a little peace in a troubled world. I sat down; the organist softly played "Silent Night"; a lighted candle burned on every window ledge. Thank God. A moment of peace.

Then the priest stood up to read the Scripture. Oh no! I couldn't believe it. He read the Scripture about "the slaughter of the innocents"— how Herod killed all the babies in Bethlehem. Blood rushed to my head. *Not on Christmas Eve!* Not to a kid who was sick of war, tragedy, evil, and bloodshed!

Then the priest said, "Jesus Christ was born into the real world—our world—a world where women and children are brutalized, where men are machine-gunned, where babies are murdered—a world riddled with sin and evil."

As I ate the bread and drank from the cup, a Spirit of joy and peace flooded my soul. My Savior came into Herod's world—our world, *my* world—to change evil into goodness, hatred into love, violence into peace, sin into salvation. I'll always remember that Holy Communion.

Let's keep Herod in Christmas to avoid sentimentality, to remember that a world saturated with sin desperately needs a Savior who can transform the human heart. Oh, if only Herod had, in fact, gone to Bethlehem to "pay him homage"! But let *us* go; let us allow the Savior to root out the evil in our world.

Issues to Ponder

Ponder for a moment your knowledge of evil. Let your historical memory focus on airplanes crashing into the Twin Towers of the World Trade Center or on a brutal murder in your town. Or picture yourself as a slave in 1840, your family members being sold on an auction block, sent to another state. Or visualize yourself as a descendant of that slave, being refused service in a café, or laughed at and turned away from a hotel late one night when you are tired and need a place to stay. Contemplate rich, powerful people deceiving the government, paying themselves outrageous bonuses, absconding with fortunes. Think about evil in the world, and consider the following questions.

Questions for Reflection and Discussion

1. Where do you think evil comes from? How does it invade the human heart? What stimulates evil, increasing its power?
2. Where, in your own life, have you experienced evil hurting you, damaging your health, your family, your resources?
3. In your inner life, where do Jesus the Savior and Herod the evil one do battle? Where are the secret seeds of sin in your heart that sometimes burst forth like weeds in spring?
4. How do you allow Jesus the Savior to help you defeat sin in your life? How do you make amends or obtain forgiveness? How does Jesus change a person's heart from evil to good?

Carol

How silently, how silently,
the wondrous gift is given;
so God imparts to human hearts

the blessings of his heaven.
No ear may hear his coming,
 but in this world of sin,
 where meek souls will receive him still,
 the dear Christ enters in.

O holy Child of Bethlehem,
 descend to us, we pray;
 cast out our sin, and enter in,
 be born in us today.
We hear the Christmas angels
 the great glad tidings tell,
 O come to us, abide with us,
 Our Lord Emmanuel!
　—Phillips Brooks, O *Little Town of Bethlehem*

Prayer

Good and gracious Savior, we know that evil creeps into our human experience like a snake in a swamp. Lying, betrayal, and violence are everywhere—outside us and inside us. Sin is in our hearts, for we "all have sinned and fall[en] short of the glory of God." May the Savior, Jesus, born in Bethlehem under King Herod's rule, be born in our hearts and live in our lives forever. And may we resist evil inside and out, the Jesus way. Amen.

LET'S KEEP THE WISE MEN IN CHRISTMAS

Scripture: Read Matthew 2:1-12.

Wisdom

WHERE CAN WISDOM BE FOUND? Let's take a look at that question as it relates to Scripture. In the Hebrew Bible (which Christians refer to as the Old Testament), wisdom can mean that an artisan, a skilled worker, knows exactly what he is doing (Exodus 36:8). Good rulers who governed well were called wise (1 Kings 3:12, 28). Sometimes wisdom was another name for simple cleverness (2 Samuel 14:2). In Proverbs, a life of prayer and godly ethical conduct is called a life of wisdom (Proverbs 2:9-11).

Traditionally, a group of books of the Bible, including Proverbs, the book of Job, and Ecclesiastes, is referred to as "Wisdom Literature." The Queen of Sheba came to visit Solomon because he was heralded to be the wisest man in the world (see 1 Kings 10:1-10). (She also wanted free trade passage to the Near East.) In the Apocrypha we find the book known as the Wisdom of Solomon. And the Psalms speak of wisdom as living a faithful, truth-speaking, righteous life.

The mouths of the righteous utter wisdom,
    and their tongues speak justice.
The law of their God is in their hearts;
    their steps do not slip. (Psalm 37:30-31)

Wisdom is often described as a "lady" in Proverbs. Over and over again she speaks, "My child, do not despise the LORD's discipline.... Happy are those who find wisdom, and those who get understanding.... She is more precious than jewels.... She is a tree of life.... The LORD by wisdom founded the earth.... My child...do not be afraid...the LORD will be your confidence" (Proverbs 3). And the key verse that perhaps summarizes the meaning of all the Proverbs is, "The fear of the LORD is the beginning of wisdom" (Proverbs 9:10).

The Wise Men

A very familiar part of the Christmas story is the three wise men. Who were these wise men who traveled to Bethlehem? In ancient times, a secular "wisdom" circled the Mediterranean: there was brilliant engineering in Egypt (as evidenced by the pyramids); profound philosophy in Greece (Plato, Aristotle, Socrates); sophisticated study of the movement of the planets and the stars in Mesopotamia, Babylonia, and Persia. The Jewish people, with their scholarship, were scattered over the known world during the *diaspora*. People traveled, and scholars read one another's scrolls. A strong religious philosophy grew up in Greece and Persia called "Gnosticism." In contrast to the persons of that time who worshiped many idols, these spiritual thinkers, "Gnostics," believed in just two gods: the god of all physical matter and the god of all spiritual matters. The wise men from the biblical Christmas story may in fact have been Gnostics from this tradition.

We know little about the wise men from the Scriptures. They were not Jews; they were foreigners, perhaps ancient Persians. Some say they were perhaps from India, students of the stars. The word *magi* is from the same root word as "magician" or "magic"; perhaps the wise men were philosopher-astronomers who studied philosophy and science. As part of their religion, these wise men paid particular attention to the movement of the stars.

Three Gifts

Just how many *magi,* or wise men, were there? We don't know; but because of the three specific gifts mentioned in Matthew, tradition quickly came to hold that there were three wise men, and soon thereafter they were given names. By the fourth century, the first of the magi, who were often also called kings, was referred to as Gaspar: he was said to have brought gold to the infant Jesus. The second wise man was named Balthazar: he gave Jesus the frankincense. The third of the *magi* was called Melchior: he brought myrrh to the manger.

The gift symbolism is powerful, even overwhelming. Gold for him who is King of kings and Lord of lords. Frankincense, used for prayer in the temple, for him who prayed all night in the garden and taught us to pray, "Our Father, who art in heaven...." Myrrh, an embalming spice, to suggest Jesus' atoning death on the cross and to remember Mary Magdalene hurrying to the tomb early on Easter morning with spices to anoint Jesus' body.

These were no ordinary gifts that the wise men brought. In biblical times, frankincense came from the sap of the *Boswellia sacra* tree grown in southern Arabia. These precious aromatics were brought to the seaport at Gaza and shipped to Europe and Egypt. Frankincense was used everywhere in worshiping the gods of different religions. Arabia produced the finest quality of frankincense and myrrh in the known world.

The Greeks used frankincense not only in their worship but also in medicine, believing that it cured chest pains, paralysis, and ulcers. It also had the practical value of preserving food and of masking the odor of cremations.

Incidentally, I've often wondered how Joseph could afford to take Mary and baby Jesus to Egypt for a couple of years and then provide for the family to travel all the way back to Nazareth in Galilee. Perhaps Joseph, a craftsman, was able to find work. But I've always believed that the gold that Gaspar brought, like manna from heaven, helped to support the holy family during that difficult period in exile. It certainly couldn't have hurt for Joseph to have a handful of gold coins in his pocket.

> Then entered in those wise men three,
> full reverently upon their knee,
> and offered there in His presence,
> their gold and myrrh and frankincense.
> —"The First Noel"

As centuries passed, artists of the church began to paint "The Magi" in a manner to represent the "entire" Gentile world: Gaspar as an old man; Balthazar as a man of middle age; and Melchior as a young man. By the ninth century, the wise men were depicted as being representative of the three continents of Europe, Asia, and—with Balthazar portrayed as having black skin—Africa. The spiritual symbolism was that the wise men represented the entirety of the non-Jewish world. The empress Helena claimed to have discovered their bones and brought them to Constantinople. Later they were moved to Milan, and today they are honored in a golden shrine in the Cologne Cathedral in Germany.

Many Christian churches celebrate Epiphany or "the Feast of Epiphany," a feast day that occurs twelve days after Christmas Day, typically on January 6 or, in some countries, on a Sunday between January 2 and January 8. The word *epiphany* literally means "showing forth," and it signifies that light has come into the world. This expression may have been rooted in ancient Egypt, where the people celebrated the birth of light following the winter solstice. The Eastern Orthodox Church uses Epiphany to remember the baptism of Jesus, the light of the world. The Western church celebrates the visitation of the wise men, remembering their pilgrimage, their delayed visit to the manger, and their Gentile, world-wide representation. Light has come into the entire world!

Gentiles

Don't underestimate the Gentile symbolism. Judaism always struggled with being a separate "Holy People" with strict religious laws on one hand, and yet belief in One Holy God of the universe, the God of all, on the other hand.

Jesus in his ministry reached out to Gentiles. Remember the demon-possessed maniac in the Gentile cemetery (Luke 8:26-33), the poor widow in Nain whose son had died (Luke 7:11-17), even the Roman soldier at the foot of the cross (Matthew 27:54). Jesus' most familiar parable, the parable of the good Samaritan (Luke 10:29-37), honors a man whose people were despised and viewed as being Gentile.

Peter, empowered by the Holy Spirit, took the gospel to the Roman centurion in Caesarea. And the apostle Paul, of course, exploded the salvation message, preaching all over the eastern Mediterranean and, crossing over, establishing Christianity in Europe.

The "wise men," Gentiles, did not know the Hebrew Scriptures fully; they did not know that the prophet Micah had foretold that the Messiah would be born in Bethlehem. They did know that King Herod had rebuilt the Temple in Jerusalem—so beautiful, so magnificent, that it was known throughout the civilized world. So they logically came, in their journey to find the newborn king of the Jews, whose birth they believed had been foretold by a star, to the center of Judaism, Jerusalem.

They must have been men of wealth and prominence. They came from afar. They must have had an entourage of servants, drivers, and animals.

Their gifts were extravagant. King Herod, who loved prominence, gave these foreign dignitaries exuberant hospitality. He called the Sanhedrin together (normally seventy Jewish leaders) to meet the foreign "kings" and to give them counsel.

The very words "the child who has been born king of the Jews" struck fear and consternation in Herod's paranoid heart. Already Herod was not well—he was sick and infirm—and some new baby was a long way from becoming king. But Herod was obsessed with power (he also wanted one of his own sons to succeed him). The wise men may have heard of Herod's reputation, and they might have been suspicious of Herod's overly enthusiastic desire to also "go and pay him homage."

Humility

Take notice that these powerful, intelligent scholar-kings were willing to listen, to take advice, and to hear Micah's prophecy (Micah 5:2). They stopped in Jerusalem to ask the way, accepted the counsel of Jewish priests and rabbis, and reestablished their trek to follow the star. In spite of their wealth and learning, they were humble! Humbly they followed the star; humbly they found their way to the Christ Child; humbly they knelt before the child with a young peasant mother and a carpenter father. Humbly and prayerfully they gave the precious gifts they had carried for hundreds of miles.

Humility in the hearts of the rich, the powerful, the intellectual elite, is a wonderful attribute. Some powerful people become haughty—too proud to associate with "the common folk." Some rich folks lavishly throw their money around in ostentatious display. Some want special privileges; they want to bend the rules in their favor.

But I have known some dynamic industrial leaders who humbly knelt to receive Holy Communion and who helped the Salvation Army and the homeless. I have watched governors sing in the choir, brilliant scholars listen attentively to a student's rather elementary questions. I have witnessed people of vast wealth giving great sums to worthy causes—secretly, silently.

The wisest people I have ever known believed in and trusted in the Lord. On a wall near my college office hangs a huge picture of Albert Einstein. Beside the picture are the words, "I want to think God's thoughts...all the rest are details." I have joined in prayer with philosophers at Yale, scientists at Duke, medical doctors in Dallas, and presidents and senators in Washington, D.C. Wise people kneel in humble gratitude before the Savior.

One of the wisest persons I ever knew was Dr. Robert Calhoun, a professor at Yale. One young, grandiose prospective Ph.D. student asked presumptuously, "Hey, Prof, how come you believe in God?" Dr. Calhoun softly and graciously (and humbly) replied, "My mother told me."

Another Way

The *magi,* after they had knelt before the Savior, after they had given their well-traveled gifts, went to sleep. They were not dummies; I believe that their experience with Herod's showy opulence and exaggerated deference helped them formulate God's message: "Being warned in a dream not to return to Herod, they departed to their own country by another way" (Matthew 2:12 RSV).

They had been to Bethlehem, they had knelt before the King of kings—and now it was time to go home. But a spiritual message resides here, like a gold coin under a rock. When we give our hearts to Jesus Christ, we go home "by another way." Our lives are forever different. Jesus said, "I am the *way,* and the truth, and the life" (John 14:6, emphasis added). His way is a different way from the ways of the world.

In today's world, some people are telling lies, while those who follow Jesus are telling the truth. Some folks are stealing, while others are honest and giving to the poor. Some adults are abusing children, while others, following Jesus, are taking children in their arms and blessing them.

Many people forget that Christian discipleship is a "way"—a way of life. Some think it is merely an act of faith: "Raise your hand if you believe in Jesus." But our Lord clearly stated, "*I am the way, and the truth, and the life.*" Again, he strongly insisted, "Not everyone who says to me 'Lord, Lord,' will enter the kingdom of heaven, but only the one who *does the will* of my Father in heaven" (Matthew 7:21, emphasis added).

So, as Christian believers, we walk a different path than our prevalent culture. The "way" means that as husbands and wives, we will not even look at others with lust (Matthew 5:27-28). We will not swear, even "on a stack of Bibles"; but our yes will be yes, and our no will be no (Matthew 5:37). Because our bodies are temples of the Holy Spirit, we will not get drunk or use drugs. Like the good Samaritan, we will give aid to the sick and the wounded, regardless of race or creed. Greed will not control our appetites, but we will feed the hungry, clothe the naked, heal the sick, visit the prison inmate (Matthew 25:35).

Recently I received a phone call from a brilliant young man with advanced university degrees. He was sophisticated, articulate. He also had just been released after serving two five-year prison terms for taking drugs and selling drugs, having begged and stolen to get them. In prison, this young man began to pray, he participated in DISCIPLE Bible Study, and he attended meetings of Kairos and Brothers in Blue. In prison, he knelt down before the Christ Child like the wise men of old. Upon his release he called me to say that he is now directing "Second Blessing"—a store of used clothing, used furniture, children's toys, and bedding for persons who are in need. He is exuberant. He says he has a "ministry." He has met Jesus, and he is going home a different way.

Like the wise men of old, once we have knelt before the Lord Jesus, we go home "by another way."

We need to keep the wise men in Christmas because they represent the people of the entire world, men and women in every continent and clime. Those "magi" teach us that no one is so far away that they cannot travel in faith to Bethlehem. Even the wealthiest and the most powerful among us need the Savior. The greatest can kneel in humility before the Lord, rise up, and serve God in faithfulness.

Issues to Ponder

1. What can I give Him,
      Poor as I am?
   If I were a shepherd
      I would bring a lamb,
   If I were a wise man
      I would do my part,—
   Yet what I can I give Him,
      Give my heart.
         —"A Christmas Carol," Christina G. Rossetti

2. Some people confuse stupidity, ignorance, or poverty, with humility. Ask yourself, what is humility?

Questions for Reflection and Discussion

1. Who do you know (or know about) who is wise, wealthy, or powerful and yet also truly humble? What is it that characterizes their humility? Why do you feel that they exhibit humility?
2. What does humility look like? Do you show it yourself? Give reasons for your answer.
3. What great lengths are you willing to go to, what great distances are you willing to travel, or what great gifts are you willing to give to Jesus Christ right now?

4. The wise men were "Gentiles"—outsiders. Do you, or does your religious fellowship, make room for outsiders, help them find the Savior, and include them in the believers' fellowship? Elaborate on your answer.

5. How would you answer the following question: Are you walking a different way from the ways of the world?

Carol

We three kings of Orient are,
Bearing gifts we traverse afar,
Field and fountain, moor and mountain,
Following yonder star.

Born a King on Bethlehem's plain,
Gold I bring to crown Him again
King forever, ceasing never,
Over us all to reign.

Frankincense to offer have I,
Incense owns a Deity nigh;
Prayer and praising, all men raising,
Worship Him, God on high.

Myrrh is mine; its bitter perfume
Breathes a life of gathering gloom;
Sorrowing, sighing, bleeding, dying,
Sealed in the stone-cold tomb.

Refrain:
O star of wonder, star of light,

Star with royal beauty bright,
Westward leading, still proceeding,
Guide us to Thy perfect light.
—John H. Hopkins, Jr., *We Three Kings*

Prayer

O Lord of all wisdom and God of the wise and the foolish, we praise you, for you are the fountain of all knowledge and the source of all truth. Save us from stupid folly, but also save us from thinking that we know all the answers. Cause us to be humble. Help us to walk in his way. Through him who is the way, the truth, and the life. Amen.

LET'S KEEP JOSEPH IN CHRISTMAS

Scripture: Read Matthew 1:18-25; 2:13-15, 19-23.

Joseph

YOU'D NOTICE HIS EYES FIRST—his eyes, and then his hands. His soft black eyes were unpretentious, without guile. He looked you straight in the eye, no furtive glances, no staring at the ground. Those eyes were accustomed to studying a plumb line dropped on a stone block wall or making sure the wooden joint was right on square.

Framed in a face leathered by the Galilean sun and wind, those eyes looked at you with an openness, a straightforwardness you immediately trusted. Yes, that would be the man you would want to carpenter your dining room table or stone-mason your home. His hands were a working man's hands, rough and beat up. Notice the broken fingernails, the calluses, the scars where a chisel had, once in a while, slipped, a hammer had hit by mistake.

Joseph was a quiet man. In all of Scripture, not a single word is recorded from Joseph's mouth. But his role in the birth and upbringing of Jesus was indispensable.

I love and respect the strong, silent type—usually men who work hard, say little, but can always be counted on. These fellows are seldom the chair of the committee, but they serve faithfully, and everyone respects their judgment, even if it's only given with a nod or a smile.

Integrity

They are men of integrity. Their word is their bond. A handshake from them is better than a signed contract. Where did Jesus learn integrity? Where did he learn "you shall not bear false witness"? Jesus taught his disciples, "Let your 'Yes' be 'Yes,' and your 'No,' 'No'; anything beyond this comes from the evil one" (Matthew 5:37 NIV). I believe Joseph was a man whose yes was yes and whose no was no.

When I was a teenager, I raised alfalfa hay and baled it, and, since I had no cattle, I sold the baled hay to farmers and ranchers. One day a quiet Mennonite farmer drove onto the field just as the baling crew left. He got out, pulled a stem of alfalfa from a bale, bit it, chewed on it, smelled the hay, and looked across the field. Then he reached out his hand and said, "I'll pay twenty dollars a ton—in the field." I shook hands. This was a good deal in those days. But as the farmer turned to go, he said, "And the dog will be in the truck."

I told my dad—who was also the strong, quiet type—what had happened. "Good," he said. "The handshake was a contract," he said. "But, Dad," I replied, "what in the world did he mean by 'the dog will be in the truck'?" Dad thought for a moment, then, sober as a judge, he said, "Son, when an empty hay truck pulls onto the scales, the scale operator notes whether the driver gets out of the cab or stays in. Then when the truck is loaded with hay, the driver will do the same. That Mennonite farmer wanted you to know that the dog will be in the truck for both weighings. That farmer won't cheat you." "Dad," I said, "I saw that dog—he must only weigh seventeen pounds. At $20 a ton, a penny a pound, that's only 17 cents." Then my father nodded and nailed it: "He's an honest man, to the penny!"

Obedience

In all of Scripture, Joseph, the husband of Mary, never says a single word. But he *listens,* and he *acts.* He hears God speak in his dreams and responds *immediately.*

When Joseph learned Mary was pregnant, he "planned to dismiss her quietly." But an angel of the Lord, in a dream, said, "Do not be afraid to take Mary as your wife," and the scriptures include an Isaiah passage that Joseph knew by heart: "The virgin shall conceive and bear a son, and they shall name him Emmanuel" (Matthew 1:19, 20, 23). Now take note of this: "When Joseph awoke from sleep, he did as the angel of the Lord commanded him; he took her as his wife" (Matthew 1:24).

That was Joseph's style: In Bethlehem, after Jesus was born, after the wise men had left, an angel of the Lord, in a dream, said, " 'Get up, take the child and his mother, and flee to Egypt.' . . . Then Joseph got up, took the child and his mother by night, and went to Egypt" (Matthew 2:13-14). Joseph *obeyed.*

Joseph must have lived close to God. When Herod died, an angel of the Lord suddenly appeared in a dream to Joseph in Egypt and said, "Get up, take the child and his mother, and go to the land of Israel." Then Joseph got up, took the child and his mother, and left Egypt. But Joseph learned that the son of Herod, Archelaus, just as brutal and violent as his father, was now ruling the Jerusalem area (Judea). Joseph again listened to God, and "after being warned in a dream, he went away to the district of Galilee" (Matthew 2:20-22).

Wow! Would that we all were *immediately obedient* to the promptings of the Lord!

Joseph and Mary were meticulously obedient to the Mosaic ritual expectations and civil laws. They made the ninety-mile journey from Nazareth to Bethlehem, probably on foot, to be registered for the census under Roman law (and therefore subject to Roman taxes). They circumcised Jesus on the eighth day, as prescribed by the law of Moses (Leviticus 12:3).

Then Joseph, without comment, took Jesus and Mary to Jerusalem for "purification" after waiting thirty-three days for Mary to finish bleeding (Luke 2:21-24; Leviticus 12:1-8). The upper and middle classes were to donate a lamb, but the poor were required to dedicate two turtledoves, and that's what Joseph did. An aged holy man, Simeon, saw Jesus, became ecstatic, and cried to God, "My eyes have seen your salvation" (Luke 2:25-30). An elderly widow, Anna, who prayed daily in the temple, saw Joseph, Mary, and Jesus and she gave thanks to God. (See Luke 2:36-38.)

But in the words of the old spiritual, Joseph stood by and "never said a mumblin' word." Then this obedient, faithful man, with Mary, parented Jesus so that "the child grew and became strong, filled with wisdom; and the favor of God was upon him" (Luke 2:40).

Joseph and Mary even brought Jesus back to Jerusalem every year, as required, for Passover (a rather hard and somewhat costly religious pilgrimage). At the age of twelve, undoubtedly by having learned Scripture at the feet of Joseph and Mary, Jesus sat with the rabbis and priests "listening to them and asking them questions. And all who heard him were amazed at his understanding and his answers" (Luke 2:46-47).

Mary and Joseph lost Jesus in the crowd. Mary reprimanded him for staying behind: "Your father and I have been searching for you in great anxiety." Joseph was silent. "Did you not know that I must be in my Father's house?" said Jesus. Jesus then went home to Nazareth with them "and was obedient to them" (Luke 2:48-51).

We never hear in the Scriptures of Joseph again. He did not attend the wedding feast in Cana. He was not with Mary and the grown children when they begged Jesus to avoid controversy in his ministry and to come home. Perhaps Joseph died when Jesus was a teenager.

Nazareth

Nazareth was a tiny town, a village. Scholars suggest that it held a few hundred people, perhaps only 150 or so. A Jewish synagogue requires ten healthy, head-of-the-family men with a rabbi. Nazareth struggled to maintain a valid, vibrant synagogue.

In a village, everybody knows everybody. No wonder Mary would have been shamed if she were pregnant without marriage. And when Jesus first spoke in his home synagogue, the local men made a typical small-town association: "Is not this Joseph's son?" (Luke 4:22). (I live in a small town myself. People refer to folks by the names of their parents, their grandparents, and even out to four generations. They remember who "used to live in that house on the corner," fifty years ago or more.)

We think of Joseph as a "carpenter." The Greek word the Bible uses, *tekton,* literally means "artisan" or "builder" or "stone mason." The King James Bible (A.D. 1611) used the word *carpenter* to describe Joseph, and so it has been ever since. Trees in Israel are in short supply: remember, Solomon imported the "cedars of Lebanon" to build the Temple in Jerusalem. Houses in Galilee are built of local limestone. Still, furniture, interior finishing, and yokes for oxen had to be built.

Maybe Joseph was an artisan, a man who could make things, fix what was broken, build houses. He knew how to use the hammer, the chisel, the plumb line, the level; Isaiah 44:13 describes the tools.

Carpenters, builders, are careful, often meticulous. A plumb line makes the wall straight; a level makes the table true. I remember when our little country church was building an addition with volunteer labor. Someone jostled the guideline string when the footings were poured. The superintendent, who was a carpenter, made us dig out the entire footing and start all over again. "It had to be right."

Picture the boy Jesus working side by side with Joseph. Listen, as the father says, "Son, it has to be perfectly straight," then perhaps adding, "That's the way God wants us to be with one another." Or hear Joseph, pointing to a builder who is constructing a house on sand, and commenting, in effect, that "when the storms come, that house will fall; it should be level and built on a solid rock foundation, the way our lives should be built on God." (Jesus taught that in Luke 6:46-49.)

Four miles from Nazareth are the ruins of the ancient city of Zippori (from the Hebrew *tzipori*, meaning "bird"), so named perhaps because that city sits on a thousand-foot-high hill, "like a bird." When the Romans conquered Israel under Pompey in 63 B.C., Zippori was made the capital of Galilee. Herod served there as district governor before going to Jerusalem. Later, after King Herod died, the Jews rioted, capturing Zippori. But soon the uprising was suppressed, and the Jews were sold into slavery. Then one of Herod's sons, Herod Antipas (one of the lucky ones who wasn't drowned by his father), began to rebuild, fortify, and modernize Zippori, restoring the city to its former status as district capital, with as many as forty thousand inhabitants, some Jews but mostly Gentiles. Today you can visit the ruins, sit on the solid stone seats in the massive open-air theater (it looks like one side of a football stadium), explore the huge aqueduct, and visit a few ancient stone houses.

Training a Teenager

Now let your historical imagination run wild. Suppose you were a craftsman, a master builder living in a tiny village. Four miles away, a large city was being constructed. The Romans were desperate for skilled workmen. So you, Joseph, take your teenage son, Jesus, and you walk or ride an ox cart daily the four miles each way, build homes and public buildings in Zippori, and walk back home where Mary and the children have supper waiting. That kind of work has happened for workers, across the centuries, everywhere.

Now, what does a father do with a thoughtful, obedient son on a typical workday? In that four-mile trek, did Jesus learn scripture? Did they talk about God? Even a quiet man would discuss important matters as they walked together: someone had cheated them on a paycheck; they were building a theater that would house plays Jews were not allowed to see; some people by the roadside had sex to sell. My quiet dad talked about things like that when I was a boy, when we worked together. My dad made ethical observations, and I bet that Joseph did too.

Jesus must also have learned a lot about life when he was exposed to Gentile culture in Zippori. In his later preaching, he used the word *hypocrite,* not an Aramaic or Hebrew word, but a Greek word meaning "actor" (from the theater). Jesus said that some religious leaders were "play acting," hypocrites. In Zippori, Jesus saw actors. He also saw poverty, sickness, persecution.

When did Joseph die? Maybe Joseph was an older man when he married Mary, perhaps a bachelor or a widower. Or maybe he died young. We do not know. The last we hear of him is when he and Mary took Jesus to celebrate the Passover in Jerusalem when Jesus was twelve. Suppose Joseph worked with Jesus for four or five more years, taught him building skills, discussed family and faith matters, then died, leaving Jesus, a teenager, to support the family. Jesus did not begin his ministry until he was thirty years old, until his younger brothers and his sister were grown and able to care for their mother. Did Jesus learn all that family integrity from Joseph?

When Jesus began his ministry, after his baptism, after his forty days and nights of fasting, prayer, and temptation in the wilderness, he came back to his hometown. At first the townspeople welcomed him—the local boy, a native son—and they asked him to speak in the little synagogue. The word *Nazareth* comes from *netzor,* meaning "the shoot of Jesse." The Nazarites had come out of exile, gathered in the farm country of Galilee, and they believed that *from them* would come the Jewish messiah to save them (the Jews). He would be a "shoot of Jesse." They were orthodox, fundamentalist, exclusive. Remember, Nathaniel, sitting under a fig tree—the sign of pondering, scholarship, theology, and independent thinking—said, "Can anything good come out of Nazareth?" (John 1:46). They believed they were "special," set apart— a people who had suffered and who had come home—a "shoot of Jesse."

Where did Jesus get the idea that God is God of the universe, of all peo- ple, of both Jews and Gentiles? Was his thinking impacted by Zippori? by Joseph? Jesus knew the words of Isaiah: "Turn to me and be saved, all the ends of the earth!" (Isaiah 45:22). And again, "I will give you as a light to the nations, that my salvation may reach to the end of the earth" (Isa- iah 49:6). Did Joseph help his son understand that people are people, and *all* are in need of salvation? The men in the little synagogue asked the local boy, Joseph's son, to read the Scriptures and to say a few words. Jesus dropped a bombshell on his conservative, down-home townsfolk.

Jesus read aloud from Isaiah 61. Then he almost "put a nail in his coffin," so to speak, by saying, "There were many widows in Israel in the time of Elijah . . . and there was a severe famine over all the land; yet Elijah was sent to none of them except to a [starving] widow at Zarephath in Sidon [a Gentile]. There were also many lepers in Israel in the time of the prophet Elisha, and none of them was cleansed except Naaman the Syrian" [the hated foreign general] (Luke 4:25-27). Joseph's fellow townsmen were inflamed, so furious that they tried to throw Jesus off a cliff; but somehow Jesus disappeared from among them (Luke 4:28- 30). I wonder what role Joseph played in helping Jesus understand God as God of all humanity.

Jesus must have learned much from his strong, quiet, hardworking father. Joseph faithfully kept Jewish religious laws and ceremonies; yet he may have worked side by side with people from all over the world. I believe that one reason our Lord was able to speak of God as heavenly Father was that he had hints of righteous, holy living from his earthly father, Joseph the carpenter.

Issues to Ponder

1. Think back. Mothers have a tremendous influence on their children, but what about fathers? What did your father or your grandfather, or another father figure in your life, say that influenced your thinking, your actions, your decisions? Was it by word, by example, or both?

2. Whether you are a father, a grandfather, an uncle, or a brother, are there children in your life who are important to you? Is your behavior guiding a child Godward? Do these children tell the truth, work hard, care about the poor, and listen to the Lord because of you? Do you take them to worship, teach them at home how to pray, or help guide them in their faith in some other positive way?

3. It is human to be suspicious of outsiders, people who are different from us—that "us" versus "them" mentality. How can we recognize that trait within ourselves, and what might we do to respond to it?

Questions for Reflection and Discussion

1. Reflect on / discuss what kind of man you think Joseph was. Do you know people like him? What traits do you see in Joseph that you admire?

2. In a world where many cheat, some lie and steal, some try to get something for nothing, some maim and kill, what can we do to encourage the Josephs of this world? Reflect on this question: Are you honest, beyond reproach?

3. Often the church includes persons who are educated, those who are socially prominent, and those in the middle class, while failing to reach those who are poor, those who lack a formal education, low-income workers, and young single parents struggling to make ends meet, for example. How can the church reach out to and include more people?

Carol

Angels we have heard on high
Sweetly singing o'er the plains,
And the mountains in reply
Echoing their joyous strains.
Gloria in excelsis Deo!

See him in a manger laid,
Whom the choirs of angels praise,
Mary, Joseph, lend your aid,
While our hearts in love we raise.
Gloria in excelsis Deo!
—traditional French carol, *Angels We Have Heard on High*

Prayer

O God, thank you for Joseph, for his willingness to listen to you and to respond promptly. Thank you for his simple virtues and for his steadfast loyalty.

O Lord, help us be a people of integrity—at home, in school, in business, and in our political lives. Help us teach our children and other youth the deep spiritual truths as they encounter a complex world. Make us open to all people, including those who are different from us. In Jesus' name. Amen.

LET'S KEEP THE SHEPHERDS IN CHRISTMAS

Scripture: Read Luke 2:8-20.

Shepherds in Ancient Israel

ABRAHAM, FATHER OF THE HEBREWS, was a shepherd, often moving about to find pasture and water, and to avoid hostile tribesmen. Abraham and his nephew, Lot, separated in order to find adequate grazing and sufficient water so their herdsmen would not quarrel (Genesis 13:8-13).

Jacob, you may remember, after cheating his brother Esau out of his birthright, slipped away in the night to a shepherd kinsman, Laban, in Haran (Genesis 29:1-5). Jacob cared for Laban's sheep for fourteen years to earn the opportunity to marry Laban's daughters, Leah and Rachel (Genesis 29:15-30).

The great prophet Amos, like a barefoot schoolboy, humbly claimed that he was a poor, uneducated shepherd (Amos 1:1).

King David, the most famous shepherd of all, worked as a boy with his father's flock near Bethlehem. He fought wild animals and, of course, is famous for his slingshot victory over the giant Goliath (1 Samuel 16:1-13; 17:1-51).

Ancient Israel was not a land of cattle ranches or hog farms. Pork was forbidden by Jewish law (Leviticus 11:7). When Jesus healed the demoniac and the demons ran into the pigs, it happened in Gentile territory (Mark 5:1-13). The practice of agriculture was scattered—some grain was grown in Galilee, along with some vineyards and fruit trees. But especially in the southern region of Judah, sheep and goats dotted the landscape. The rocky hills from Jerusalem to Hebron and Bethlehem housed constantly migrating sheep and goats. The soil was so shallow, the rocky outcroppings so profuse, the rain so occasional, the grass so sparse, that the sheep and the goats moved continually. The old proverb said, "They have to sharpen the sheeps' noses so they can ferret out the grass from between the rocks."

So in ancient Palestine, shepherding was prominent, essential. Sheep were the mainstay of the inhabitants' livelihood. Sheep provided wool, meat, clothing, and material for tents. Lambs were regularly laid on the altar in Jerusalem's Temple as a spiritual sacrifice. Jesus saw plenty of shepherds in his lifetime.

The Christmas Shepherds

In springtime, during the day, shepherds and families who owned the sheep had much to do. They worked hard, assisting in the birthing of new lambs, caring for those little ones. Amid strong winds and spring rains, they sheared the sheep, harvested the winter wool, and readied the ewes and bucks for summer weather. They butchered young males and castrated others for later meat supply. They took a firstborn lamb to the Temple as a sacrificial thank offering. Of course, like the shepherd boy David, they were on the alert for wild animals, foxes, bears, even lions, critters energized by spring, hungry for a newborn lamb or an errant billy goat.

Summer was more laid back. When my wife and I visited the pastures near Bethlehem a few years ago, we saw mothers watching the sheep graze. The women were visiting under a tree, keeping an eye on their children, who were laughing and playing all around the flock. Of course, fewer wild animals were prowling around then than in Bible times.

Wintertime is different, both then and now. The sheep ranchers—the owners—would feed their sheep a little hay, maybe a bit of grain, move them about on dried-up pasture, then go home to eat supper with their families. At nighttime in winter, in the pasture, in the cold, there was little to do: build a campfire, perhaps sing a song to help quiet the sheep and to keep the wild animals at bay. The hired hands were called shepherds, but at night, in winter, their main job was to bed down the sheep, perhaps in a cave, often around a fire, then go to sleep, leaving one fellow awake to watch. The owners were in their homes, asleep, along with their wives and children.

So these nighttime winter shepherds were the poorest of the poor. They owned nothing, couldn't get a decent-paying daytime job, and often had neither home nor family. Now, let your imagination work: One of these shepherds is a war veteran, who has a limp in his left leg and no left arm; another is an old man, nearly blind, who has been around sheep all his life; over there is another shepherd, a sixteen-year-old boy who is possibly physically or mentally challenged but able to toss a stick on the fire or hum a song between 2:00 and 3:00 A.M. These nighttime hired hands, minimum-salary shepherds, were considered, in that day and time, to be at the bottom of the social ladder.

So the Christmas angels sang, as J. Ellsworth Kalas writes, not to "jeweled women in box seats." Hired-hand shepherds were so poor that they often had a bad reputation. According to Leon Morris, they had an "unfortunate habit of confusing 'thine' with 'mine' as they moved about the country." The shepherds were not allowed to give testimony in the courts in those days; they were usually considered unreliable (Leon Morris, *Luke* [Downers Grove, Ill.: InterVarsity Press, 1988] page 34).

I don't know why the angels came first to the shepherds. I've always wondered why these humble night workers got to the manger before the wise men. (Some say that uneducated, simple people come more easily to faith than wise people and scholars who have to work through a lot of thought problems before they come to the Lord. Is that true?)

When the heavens opened and a multitude of angels sang "Hallelujah, Hallelujah, Praise the Lord"; when the skies were aflame with glory and God was announcing to the universe that the Savior of the world lay in a crib in Bethlehem:

King Herod was asleep.

The Roman generals were asleep.

The rich merchants, the lawyers, the teachers, and the priests were asleep.

God chose to have the angels sing to these humble folk, these shepherds, the weakest of the weak, the loneliest of the lonely, the poorest of the poor!

The first word out of the angel's mouth was, "Do not be afraid." Luke says the shepherds were "terrified." That's understandable—lonely shepherds standing around a tiny campfire night after night, listening to the wind, staring at the stars—they would be shocked out of their sandals by a heavenly host singing the Hallelujah Chorus and by an angel speaking directly to them!

> The angel said to them, "Do not be afraid; for see—I am bringing you good news of great joy ... to you is born this day in the city of David a Savior, who is the Messiah, the Lord." (Luke 2:10-11)

Christmas is wrapped up in miracles. Martin Luther said the greatest miracle of Christmas was that when the angel told Mary she was to bear a child, the Savior, "*Mary believed.*" Of similar size is another miracle: the shepherds believed! They said, "Let us go now to Bethlehem and see this thing...which the Lord has made known to us" (Luke 2:15-16).

So they went with haste. They obeyed the heavenly vision.

Some people hear an angel speaking and keep on tending the sheep. Some of us hear heaven singing and we throw another stick on the fire.

The shepherds hurried to the manger.

Some people avoid barnyards. They shy away from the hay and the dirt. They shun the smell of cow dung and ox urine.

But the shepherds knew animal shelters. They were more at home with animal odors and floors of dirt than they were with stone homes. They were not deterred by the angelic instruction, "You will find a child wrapped in bands of cloth and lying in a manger" (Luke 2:12).

I wish I could have been there when the shepherds crept in, quiet, respectful, curious. I wish I could have seen the look in Joseph's eyes, the glance from Mary, the gurgle from the baby Jesus. Nothing is more exciting than to walk into a birth room, see a newborn baby, and, from deep in one's heart, say, "Ooh, isn't that child precious!"

The shepherds sensed that something tumultuous was happening in their souls. They were being brought into the presence of God.

No verse in Scripture is more exciting, more fulfilling, than "The shepherds returned, glorifying and praising God for all they had heard and seen" (Luke 2:20).

Our God has a special heart for the humble. Those who are poor are not blocked by prestige or wealth but are often open to the eternal. Stripped of everything earthly, they sometimes reach out to the heavenly! Jesus looked at the wealthy, the leaders, the self-righteous and said, "The tax collectors and the prostitutes are going into the kingdom of God ahead of you" (Matthew 21:31). Historically great Christian revival movements have started among the poor: Saint Francis's going to the poor in Italy; John Wesley's preaching to the peasants and prisoners in England; William Booth's offering Christ to the "ragtag and bobtail" of London to start the Salvation Army.

A miracle of Christmas is that the angels sang first to the shepherds, that they hurried to the manger, and that they believed and returned to the fields, glorifying God.

Jesus, the Good Shepherd

The imagery of God caring for Israel as "shepherd" permeates the Old Testament. Psalm 80 opens with a prayer request: "Give ear, O Shepherd of Israel, you who lead Joseph like a flock!...Stir up your might, and come to save us!" (Psalm 80:1-2).

Isaiah affirms the tender, protective care God shows Israel: "He will feed his flock like a shepherd; he will gather the lambs in his arms, and carry them in his bosom, and gently lead the mother sheep" (Isaiah 40:11).

Jesus said, "I am the good shepherd. I know my own and my own know me" (John 10:14). Jesus even enlarged his flock: "I have other sheep that do not belong to this fold. I must bring them also...there will be one flock, one shepherd" (John 10:16).

Hired hands, like nighttime shepherds, might run away in the face of armed thieves or wild animals, but Jesus said, "The good shepherd lays down his life for the sheep" (John 10:11). As his disciples, we know that he loves us and calls us personally by name. He gave up his life for us on Calvary's cross, as well expressed in Isaac Watts's hymn:

> Alas! and did my Savior bleed, and did my Sovereign die?
> Would he devote that sacred head for sinners such as I?

In my bed at night, I often silently say the Twenty-third Psalm, sometimes called David's psalm. Jesus knew it by heart. Here's how I say it: The Lord Jesus is my Good Shepherd. I shall never be in want. I am so blessed. He lets me rest where the lush pastures are green (I've never missed a meal). He does not take me beside rushing, dangerous waters (where a sheep could fall in and drown), but he leads me beside still waters. If I get bumped on the head or get thorns in my scalp, he puts my head on his lap and gently removes the thorns; he puts healing oil on the cuts. He knows the trails, for he is the Way. He does not lead me into sinful or dangerous paths of evil where sin and trouble lurk, but he leads me in the right, the "righteousness" path. So I fear not, I fear not the Evil One, for the Lord is with me. I will eat at his table, drink from his cup, and one day I will live in his heavenly home forever!

Jesus, Savior for the Poor Today

Almighty God did not take a loaf of bread or a cup of hot tea to the shepherds. He did more. God announced the birth of the Savior, led them to the manger, helped them kneel before the Lord Jesus, then sent them back into the field, their hearts singing for joy.

I've been in the church a long time. I've helped with food programs, raised money for overseas relief, and given used clothes to the Salvation Army. I support Habitat for Humanity and Heifer International, whose mission is to end hunger and poverty. But neither I nor my Christian friends often invite those who are poor to the church or to the Savior. In all societies, including ours, a social barrier, high as the Great Wall of China, separates the upper and middle classes from the poor and indigent. The migrant worker at the chicken plant, the young person behind the counter at the local fast-food restaurant, the inmate in prison, the person who sleeps under the bridge—these folks are hard for us to reach for Jesus. We are often aloof and distant; they are sometimes suspicious and defensive. But Jesus went to the poor, the marginalized, the outcast: "Blessed are you who are poor, for yours is the kingdom of God" (Luke 6:20).

Remember the woman who had hemorrhaged for twelve years and who "had spent all she had on physicians"? She touched Jesus' garment and she was healed (Luke 8:43-48). Picture the man, blind from birth, sitting squat-legged, barefoot and haggard, cup in hand, crying out,

"Alms, alms, please." Our Lord asked, "What do you really want?" When the man said, "I want to see again," Jesus gave him his sight (see Mark 10:46-52).

Perhaps the most dramatic encounter was Jesus' passing through Samaria on his way from Jerusalem to Galilee. While the disciples went into town for food at lunchtime, Jesus deliberately sat down by Jacob's Well and spoke to a Samaritan woman. The Samaritans were despised by the Jews, rebellious of Judean authority, and looked down upon as modifiers of Hebrew law. All the women of the village carried their water from the community well early in the morning or at evening time, going to and from the well in the coolest parts of the day. This particular Samaritan woman got her water at noon instead, isolated and alone. Jesus correctly said that she had been married five times and was now living with a man who was not her husband. Socially speaking, she was in the company of the shepherds when the village women wouldn't even gossip with her at morning water-carrying. Jesus graciously gave to her the water of everlasting life. And with a heart full of joy, she ran to tell the entire village, with the same joy that exploded in the shepherd's hearts when they left the manger (John 4:4-29).

When I was about fifteen, Mom and Dad asked me to take some food to a woman whose husband had just died. I could drive. *It shouldn't take long,* I thought, since I had other things to do. I looked at the address—it was in the poorest part of town. On arriving, I saw a rundown shack of a house. I stepped onto a creaky porch, knocked on the door, then knocked again, and heard nothing. My teenage interior motor was running, so I turned to leave, only to hear a rustling noise and a voice from inside.

A very old woman, limping with a cane, opened the door and welcomed me in. She took the plate of food, eyes glistening, and she began to praise God and express gratitude for my thoughtful parents, and for me. She said, "A busy young man, taking time to come and see me!" I was embarrassed, standing first on one foot, then the other, when she said, "Let's pray." Before I knew it, she was on her knees, glorifying God for his blessings, thanking God that "such a busy young man" would take the time to bring her food. When I left, I was walking on air, having visited one of the poorest of the poor, celebrating the saving grace of God.

Once when Jesus was eating with the religious leaders, the Hebrew lawyers, and the Pharisees, noticing how they gave prestigious places at the table to honored guests, he taught: "When you give a banquet, invite the poor, the crippled, the lame, and the blind. And you will be blessed, because they cannot repay you, for you will be repaid at the resurrection of the righteous" (Luke 14:13-14).

So, let's keep the shepherds in Christmas. Let's remember that the angels sang first to the poorest of the poor. Let's recall that these humble boys and men obeyed: "Let us go now to Bethlehem." Let us never forget that they went back to the field, full of joy, glorifying God in the birth of their Savior. Let us adore and follow the Good Shepherd. And let us never forget the poor—in our towns, in our land, and in our world, and may we help them find Jesus.

While Shepherds Watched Their Flocks

> While shepherds watched their flocks by night,
> all seated on the ground,
> the angel of the Lord came down,
> and glory shone around,
> and glory shone around.
>
> "Fear not!" said he, for mighty dread
> had seized their troubled mind.
> "Glad tidings of great joy I bring

45

> to all of humankind,
> to all of humankind."
> —Nahum Tate

Issues to Ponder

Who are the poor in your community? Is your church reaching them for Jesus?

Questions for Reflection and Discussion

1. Often we, as individuals, can do little to lessen the causes of poverty, but sometimes we can. Can you think of anything you can do to attack the *causes*?
2. Right at home, we can help minister to those who are poor. Do you strengthen your community food programs? Do you provide used clothing to the Salvation Army? Do you volunteer at soup kitchens? Where do you see particular, identifiable needs in your town or community; and what steps can you take to help?
3. The shepherds went to Jesus. One failure of Christian churches is to give food but not saving grace, clothing but not Christian fellowship, to the poor and outcast. What could you do to help them hear the angels sing, help them find the manger of Bethlehem, help them find salvation in the church?

Carol

> The first Noel the angel did say
> was to certain poor shepherds
> in fields as they lay;
> in fields where they

lay keeping their sheep,
on a cold winter's night
that was so deep.

Noel, Noel! Noel, Noel!
Born is the King of Israel!
—traditional English carol, *The First Noel*

Prayer

Lord Jesus, we thank you that you have a special heart for those who are poor. We are grateful that the angels sang first to the shepherds in the field on a cold winter night. Help us to kneel before the Savior. Help us to remember the poor, the lonely, the outcast. Help us give not only food and shelter, but saving grace and fellowship. Amen.

Made in the USA
Middletown, DE
03 December 2021

54164469R00029